Faceless Digital Course Creation: 14-Day Start-to-Finish Action Plan

(No Self Audio-Video Recording)

Beginner's 1 Digital Course Every 14 Days Blueprint. Build a Side Hustle with a Steady Income Stream

Simon E. Lee

Disclaimer

"This book is intended for informational and educational
purposes only. The information presented in this book is
not a substitute for professional financial or legal advice.
The author and publisher make no representations or
warranties of any kind, express or implied, about the
completeness, accuracy, reliability, sustainability, or
availability of the book or the information, products,
services, or related graphics contained in the book for any

Dedication

This book, "Faceless Digital Course Creation: 14-Day Start to Finish Action Plan (No Self Audio-Video Recording Required)," is wholeheartedly dedicated to the visionaries and innovators who have revolutionized the realm of educational content creation and delivery. At the forefront of this transformation are the AI-powered scriptwriting tools, Text-to-Speech (TTS) technologies, and audio-to-video creation platforms that have democratized the art of digital education. These tools have simplified processes and opened doors to countless individuals, offering opportunities that were once gated behind complex barriers.

We sincerely thank the developers and thinkers behind AI-powered tools like ChatGPT4, which have become cornerstones in crafting engaging and accessible educational content. Their groundbreaking work in natural language processing and machine learning has laid the groundwork for a new era of education, one where knowledge is not just imparted but is made to resonate with learners of diverse backgrounds and capabilities. These tools have enhanced the efficiency of course creation and injected a level of inclusivity and customization previously unimagined.

Furthermore, this dedication is to the creators of AI-powered online course platforms, who have meticulously crafted spaces where learning is not just a transaction but an experience. Their platforms are the stages upon which the symphony of AI-assisted content comes to life, reaching audiences far and wide. This book is a celebration of these technological advancements and a testament to the belief that education, in its most engaging and innovative form, should be accessible to all. Here's to the ongoing journey of breaking down barriers and opening up a world of limitless educational possibilities.

Acknowledgments

This work is a tribute to the extraordinary efforts of visionary tech developers, the brilliant minds behind AI tools, and the architects of AI-powered platforms for digital course delivery. Their tireless dedication and innovative spirit have not only reshaped the landscape of education but have also paved the way for new horizons in knowledge dissemination. A special acknowledgment is owed to the developers of ChatGPT and Bard, whose contributions have significantly enriched the domain of AI-assisted communication and learning. Their creations exemplify the pinnacle of progress in AI technology, bridging gaps and fostering connections in ways that were once the mere stuff of dreams. Their work is a beacon that guides us toward a future where education is more accessible, engaging, and tailored to the needs of learners worldwide.

On a personal note, I extend my deepest and most heartfelt gratitude to my charming wife, whose unwavering support and culinary prowess have been my steadfast companions through the countless hours dedicated to this endeavor. Her ability to nourish the body and spirit with her healthy culinary creations has been a source of comfort and strength. Her presence has been a reminder of the beautiful balance between technological advancements and the warmth of human touch. Her support has been a cornerstone in my journey to spread the word about the myriad income avenues unlocked by the AI revolution. These avenues promise to enrich lives and broaden horizons.

I offer my profound thanks to all these individuals, both in the forefront and behind the scenes. Your collective genius and compassion have made this work possible and ignited a spark that will illuminate the path for many who seek to explore the vast and ever-expanding realm of digital education. Your contributions are a testament to the power of collaboration, innovation, and the relentless pursuit of making the world a more knowledgeable and connected place.

Preface

This book, born from a deep-seated mission to illuminate the vast landscape of opportunities heralded by the AI Revolution, is more than just a guide; it's a beacon of hope and empowerment. In a world where the relentless march of technology often sparks apprehension, particularly around job security, the democratizing power of AI emerges as a counterbalance, a tool for liberation and growth. Living in an era and in countries where freedom fosters innovation, this book aims to accelerate the positive impact of AI among the masses. It's an effort to communicate, educate, and open doors to possibilities once locked away in the realms of specialists and tech aficionados.

The essence of this book is rooted in the belief that anyone, regardless of their background or experience with technology, can harness the potential of AI-powered tools to not just adapt but thrive in an ever-evolving job market. It's crafted for the absolute beginner, those who might feel overwhelmed by the rapid technological advancements and are searching for a tangible, accessible path to reinvent themselves. Over a few days or weeks, readers will journey through learning and mastering AI tools — tools that are not merely gadgets of convenience but powerful instruments for creating new income streams and opportunities. This book is for those displaced by AI, offering them not just solace but practical solutions; it's a guide to turning what many perceive as a threat into an avenue for personal and professional growth.

Disclaimer

In this 14-day action plan, we recommend a specific set of AI-powered tools that we found effective and user-friendly for creating faceless digital course videos. These recommendations are based on our research and experience and are intended to streamline the learning and creation process for beginners. It is important to note that there are numerous tools available in the market, each with its unique features and capabilities. Our selection is not an exhaustive list, nor is it an endorsement of these tools as the only or the best options available.

If you are already familiar with or are using different tools that serve similar purposes, we encourage you to continue using them. The principles and strategies outlined in our action plan are adaptable and can be applied using various tools that offer similar functionalities. Our aim is to provide a structured and straightforward path for beginners who may not have prior knowledge or experience with these tools. For such individuals, our recommended tools can serve as a valuable starting point, saving time and reducing the complexity of navigating the vast landscape of digital content creation tools.

The world of AI-powered education and informative digital content creation is dynamic and constantly evolving. We recommend staying informed about the latest developments and exploring different tools as you grow and refine your skills in digital course creation.

Table of Contents

Introduction

"AI has the potential to transform education by making it more personalized,

effective and accessible." - **Melinda Gates**

Imagine you could create engaging and informative

digital courses without ever appearing on camera or

recording your voice. This is the power of AI-powered
faceless digital courses, a revolutionary approach to
education that is transforming the way people learn and
share knowledge.

In the age of AI-powered productivity tools, it's no surprise that education is also undergoing a digital transformation. Faceless digital courses are gaining popularity because they offer a convenient, personalized, and engaging learning experience for students of all ages and backgrounds.

What is an AI-powered Faceless Digital Course (No self audio-video required)

But what exactly is an AI-powered faceless digital course? It's a type of online course that uses artificial intelligence (AI) to generate voiceovers, animations, and other multimedia elements, allowing instructors to create high-quality content without ever showing their faces or speaking into a microphone.

This innovative approach to education offers several advantages and benefits, including:

Increased accessibility: Faceless digital courses make learning content production and delivery more accessible to people who may be shy or uncomfortable on camera or those who have physical limitations that make traditional video recording difficult.

Personalized learning: AI tools can analyze individual student performance and adapt the course content accordingly, providing a more personalized and effective learning experience.

Engaging content: AI-powered animations and voiceovers can make course content more engaging and interactive, keeping students motivated and focused.

Reduced production costs: Creating faceless digital courses is often less expensive than traditional video courses, as it eliminates the need for expensive equipment and studio rentals.

The opportunities for AI-powered faceless digital courses are endless. From teaching academic subjects to providing vocational training, these courses can be used to educate and empower people of all ages and backgrounds, regardless of their location or physical limitations.

If you're a content creator, entrepreneur, or educator looking to create engaging and impactful learning experiences and do not necessarily like to use your own voice or show your face on the video camera, then AI-powered faceless digital courses are the perfect solution for you.

Join the revolution in education and discover the power of AI to transform the way people learn.

Chapter 1 - Day 1: Digital Course Creation Terms and Online Course Platforms

" "The intersection of AI and education is where the true gold lies.". - Satya Nadella, CEO of Microsoft:

Welcome to the fascinating world of faceless digital course creation, where you can share your knowledge and expertise without ever appearing on camera.

The main topics in this Day-1 Chapter 1 are:

1. Getting familiar with digital course creation terms
2. Online course platforms

Getting Familiar with Key Terminologies You Would Likely Encounter As You Get Deeper Into Digital Course Creation.

We have compiled a comprehensive list of 75 terms (and their definitions) that relate to major sections of the start-to-finish process of creating and producing faceless digital video courses:

- AI-powered Tools for Course Development

- Script Writing and Editing

- Content Conversion to Audio and Video

- E-learning and Digital Marketing

Check out the Glossary of Terms towards the back of this book that lists the definitions of these 75 essential terms. We strongly encourage you to get familiar with these terminologies. Below, however, are some key terms that we think you should get exposed to from the get-go.

AI-powered faceless digital course: An online course that utilizes artificial intelligence (AI) to create voiceovers, animations, and other multimedia elements, allowing instructors to create high-quality content without ever showing their faces or speaking into a microphone.

Voiceover: A voice recording that is played over a video or audio track. In AI-powered faceless digital courses, voiceovers are typically generated using AI tools like Speechify.

Animation: A sequence of images that are displayed in rapid succession to create the illusion of movement. In AI-powered faceless digital courses, animations are often used to enhance the visual appeal and engagement of the content.

Multimedia: A combination of different media formats, such as text, images, audio, and video. AI-powered faceless digital courses often make use of multimedia to create a more immersive and engaging learning experience.

Platform: An online hosting service that provides the infrastructure and tools for creating and managing an online course. Popular platforms for AI-powered faceless digital courses include Kajabi, Teachable, Thinkific, LearnWorlds, and others.

Topic selection: The process of choosing a subject or theme for your AI-powered faceless digital course.

Content research: The process of gathering information and resources for your AI-powered faceless digital course.

Tools: Software applications that can be used to create and edit AI-powered faceless digital courses. Popular tools include Lumen5 and Speechify.

Review And Comparison of Online Course Platforms

There are many options available when choosing an online course platform. The various factors to consider include features offered by different platforms, pricing, customer reviews, and support.

- It is also important to distinguish between standalone online course platforms which are a smaller branch of the bigger online learning platforms that include WordPress plugins for online courses and course marketplaces like Skillshare and Udemy.

- Platforms like LearnWorlds, Thinkific, Teachable, and Kajabi are standalone options, and they each offer unique features and benefits.

- WordPress plugins such as WP CourseWare, LearnDash, and LifterLMS, on the other hand, can be integral for those who prefer integrating course management into their existing WordPress sites.

- On the concept of course marketplaces, you have platforms like Skillshare, Udemy, LinkedIn

Learning, and Coursera. These platforms not only allow the creation and hosting of courses but also provide a vast audience, which can be beneficial for course visibility and enrollment.

Overall, the importance of carefully evaluating each platform's offerings to find the one that best aligns with the instructor's goals, whether for coaching, teaching, or corporate training. This approach ensures that the selected platform effectively meets the specific requirements and preferences of the course creator.

Why Teachable Is Uniquely Suitable For The Beginner Venturing Into The AI-Powered Faceless Digital Course Side Hustle

It is time to review the popular platforms for hosting your AI-powered faceless digital course. Each has its own strengths and weaknesses. Our review is not exhaustive; there are many other, as we indicated above, platforms out there. Here's a comparison of 4 popular platforms.

Kajabi:

Kajabi is a comprehensive platform that offers a wide range of features, including course creation tools, marketing automation, and payment processing. It's a good option for instructors who want a one-stop shop for managing their entire online course business. Kajabi helps people turn their knowledge into a sustainable online business by diversifying their revenue streams with digital products and services, including (but not limited to) online courses, online communities, and coaching programs.

Teachable:

Teachable is a more focused platform that prioritizes ease of use and course creation. It's a good option for instructors who are just starting out and want a simple platform to get them up and running quickly. The idea behind Teachable is to make it easier to create and sell knowledge products. You don't need to do any coding or have any technical skills to get started. All you have to do is sign up and use the drag-and-drop course creator to put together your curriculum and lessons. Then, set your pricing and start selling using the built-in marketing and sales tools.

Thinkific

Thinkific is a software platform that enables entrepreneurs to create, market, sell, and deliver their own online courses. Their published mission is to revolutionize the way people learn and earn online by giving them the tools they need to turn their expertise into a sustainable business that impacts both them and their audience. Thinkific is designed to facilitate building, marketing, and selling online courses, so its platform comes pre-loaded with tools that simplify the entire process from end to end.

LearnWorlds

LearnWorlds is a powerful, easy-to-use, and reliable training solution for individuals and enterprises. A fully customizable, white-label solution to train employees and associates, educate customers, or sell online courses to a wide audience. LearnWorlds enables its users to create a whole e-learning website, author online courses, and provides the tools to market & sell them both as B2B and B2C products.

Why Teachable?

For this action plan to create a digital course every 14 days, we considered features in the online platform that will save the beginner valuable time and effort in addition to being efficient. If you are using another platform already, by all means, stick with it. Ours is only a recommendation, and it is exhaustive. Even the beginners are, of course, free to choose another online course platform that, in their view, is better suited for them.

Teachables' AI-Powered Course Curriculum Generator

The inclusion of Teachable's AI-powered course curriculum generator further enhances its appeal, especially for beginners in digital course creation.

Teachable's integration of an AI-powered course curriculum generator marks a significant advancement in simplifying the course creation process. This feature harnesses the power of AI to provide immediate, practical assistance in generating a course outline, a task that can often be daunting for beginners.

By simply entering a brief description of the intended course, users can receive a well-structured outline in mere moments. This capability not only saves time but also provides a solid starting point for course development, making the initial steps of creating a course less overwhelming.

The generated outline serves as a foundational framework upon which creators can build and customize their courses. Teachable's flexible curriculum builder allows for easy rearranging, editing, and personalization of the content. This level of customization ensures that while the AI provides a significant head start in terms of structure and organization; the creator retains full control over the final content and presentation of the course.

This blend of AI-assisted efficiency and personal creative freedom makes Teachable a particularly appealing platform for those looking to streamline the course development process while still maintaining a unique and individualized approach to their course content.

Teachable stands out as a premier platform for beginners interested in creating and selling digital courses thanks to its user-friendly design and comprehensive features.

Here's A Summary Highlighting Why Teachable Might Be Particularly Suitable For Beginners:

Ease of Use: Teachable is celebrated for its beginner-friendly interface, making it simple for newcomers to navigate through course creation and management. Its intuitive design requires no technical expertise, allowing creators to focus more on the content rather than grappling with complex software.

All-in-One Platform: Teachable offers an expansive range of tools in a single package. It handles everything from web hosting to payment processing, significantly reducing the technical workload for course creators. This all-inclusive approach is particularly beneficial for beginners who may not have the resources or skills to manage multiple aspects of digital course creation independently.

Creative Freedom and Customization: Unlike some course-building platforms that limit user control, Teachable offers more options and freedom in terms of course design and content. This flexibility is crucial for creators who wish to infuse their courses with personal branding and unique teaching styles.

Free Plan Availability: Teachable's free plan is an excellent starting point for beginners. It allows creators to experiment with the platform and start building their courses without any initial investment. This plan includes key features like unlimited students, product creation, and basic quizzes, providing a solid foundation for new course creators.

Guided Course Creation: For those creating their first course, Teachable offers a detailed system that guides users through the process. This step-by-step assistance is invaluable for beginners, ensuring they understand each aspect of course creation and can learn as they build.

Cost-Effective Pricing Plans: Teachable's pricing plans are structured to cater to various levels of course creation, from hobbyists to growing businesses. While it is more expensive compared to some alternatives, the absence of transaction fees in its higher-tier plans can be more economical in the long run for creators generating substantial sales.

In summary, Teachable's blend of ease of use, comprehensive features, creative flexibility, and supportive structure for beginners makes it an attractive option for those new to digital course creation.

Its free plan and scalable pricing models also ensure that creators can start small and expand as their business grows, making it a viable and sustainable choice for building a successful course business.

Links To Popular Online Course Platforms We Discussed In This Chapter. Feel Free To Explore Them And Others Not Included Below

Kajabi.com

Teachable.com

Thinkific.com

Learnworlds.com

Chapter 2 - Day 2: Idea Generation, AI Curriculum Script Writing Tool

"AI in education can democratize access to quality learning." - Daphne Koller, Co-founder of Coursera

Embark on the exciting journey of crafting compelling scripts for your faceless digital course. In this chapter, you'll discover the power of Jasper, a cutting-edge AI writing tool, to brainstorm and generate content ideas that will captivate your audience. Learn essential script writing techniques to ensure your scripts are clear, concise, and engaging, perfectly suited for the natural-sounding audio narration produced by Speechify. By the end of this chapter, you'll be equipped with the skills to transform your ideas into captivating scripts that will form the foundation of your successful faceless digital course.

Chapter 2 runs for two days, day 2 and 3, of this AI-powered faceless digital course creation journey and covers:

- Course idea brainstorming and generation and,

- Getting familiar with the AI-powered curriculum content writing tools

For these tasks, Jasper and Grammarly will be the front-and-center AI-powered tools that will help streamline the workflow. Jasper, your AI-powered writing assistant, will also be your go-to tool for brainstorming and developing content ideas.

Strategies For Effective Generation And Selection Of Compelling Topics For Your Digital Court Target Audience.

These five guideposts present an insightful and strategic approach to creating successful online courses. It emphasizes the importance of aligning course topics with the instructor's passion and expertise, which is crucial for engaging and inspiring students. The guide outlines a five-step process for course creation:

Embracing Your Expertise and Passion: This step focuses on identifying personal interests and areas of expertise, which is essential for creating content that resonates with both the instructor and the audience. By blending passion with knowledge, instructors can create more compelling and authentic courses.

Navigating Market Demand and Riding the Trends: This involves researching market trends and demands to ensure the course topic is relevant and sought after. Staying attuned to current trends and societal needs can help in creating courses that address gaps in the market.

Surpassing Competitors and Forging Your Unique Path: Here, the guide suggests conducting competitor analysis to identify unique selling points and differentiators. Understanding what others offer allows instructors to fill market gaps and tailor their courses to meet specific learner needs.

Understanding Your Audience and Meeting Their Desires: Creating learner personas and conducting audience analysis are vital for tailoring content to meet the specific needs and preferences of the target audience. This step ensures that the course is relevant and addresses the actual challenges faced by learners.

Aligning Your Course Topic with Your Goals and Ambitions: The final step involves aligning the course topic with personal and professional goals, ensuring that teaching the course also supports the instructor's growth and development.

Overall, this guide provides a well-rounded approach to online course creation, emphasizing the importance of passion, market understanding, unique positioning, audience insights, and personal alignment.
These elements are key to creating impactful and successful online courses that not only impart knowledge but also foster community and engagement.

Tips for Effective Content Research

Gathering high-quality content is essential for creating an informative and engaging AI-powered faceless digital course. Here are some tips for effective content research:

- **Identify reliable sources:** Stick to credible sources like academic journals, industry publications, and reputable websites.

- **Gather diverse perspectives:** Consult multiple sources to gain a comprehensive understanding of your topic.

- **Verify information:** Fact-check all information before including it in your course.

- **Organize your findings:** Keep your research materials organized and easily accessible.

Idea Brainstorming And Generation With Jasper

Jasper AI is a system of artificial intelligence called Jasper that has been created to offer sophisticated language processing capabilities. Based on a given stimulus, it is intended to comprehend and produce text that resembles that of a human. Deep learning techniques are used by Jasper AI, which has been trained on enormous volumes of text data to produce responses that are logical and appropriate for the given context.

The ability of Jasper AI to comprehend and respond to a variety of prompts and questions is one of its primary characteristics. It is capable of producing text that is coherent, pertinent to the situation, and interesting. The model can offer insightful and precise responses across a variety of fields because it has been trained on a wide range of topics. Moreover, Jasper AI is capable of engaging in dynamic and interactive dialogues because it can modify its responses based on the circumstances.

Jasper's advanced AI capabilities can help you quickly generate a plethora of topic ideas and even provide initial script outlines or even full script drafts. This is particularly beneficial for beginners who are still gaining confidence in their scriptwriting skills.

Here's How to Effectively Utilize Jasper And Other AI Tools For Idea Generation And Brainstorming

- **Understanding Your Audience:** Start by defining your target audience. Understanding their interests, challenges, and learning goals can guide you in generating relevant course ideas.

- **Provide Jasper with a starting point:** Give Jasper a brief description of your course topic or a specific question you want to address in your lesson. In Jasper, input basic details about your target audience and the broad subject area you're interested in.

- **Choose the appropriate Jasper template:** Select the "Blog Post Ideas" or "Content Generator" template to generate a list of relevant topic ideas or script outlines. Also, experiment with Jasper's templates for blog post ideas or content outlines. Although these are typically used for articles, they can spark ideas for course topics.

- **Refine and expand on Jasper's suggestions:** Review Jasper's suggestions and select the ones that resonate with you. Use these as the foundation for your own research and content development.

Experiment with different prompts to generate a wider range of ideas. Adjust your inputs based on trends, industry needs, or specific skills your audience wants to learn.

- **Generating Course Ideas with Other Tools:** Tools like BuzzSumo can provide insights into trending topics in your field. Google Trends can help identify what people are searching for in your subject area.

The Iterative Process of Course Creation

Remember, course creation is an iterative process. Continually refine and update your course based on student feedback and learning outcomes.

By leveraging AI tools for both idea generation and course structuring, you can create comprehensive, engaging, and well-organized online courses that resonate with your target audience. Jasper helps in brainstorming and conceptualizing course ideas, while Teachable's curriculum generator and other AI-powered features provide a solid structural foundation for your course, which you can then customize and perfect.

Script Essentials

When crafting scripts for your AI-powered faceless digital course, keep these essential elements in mind:

- Clarity: Ensure your script is clear, concise, and easy for viewers to follow. Use simple language and avoid jargon.

- Engagement: Captivate your audience with a conversational tone, storytelling elements, and relevant examples.

- Structure: Organize your script into a logical sequence, using transition words and phrases to guide viewers through the content.

- Pacing: Maintain a consistent pace that keeps viewers engaged without overwhelming them.

Writing Tips for Engaging Course Curriculum Scripts

Here are some additional tips for writing compelling scripts that are suitable for Teachable's course curriculum structure.

- Use active voice: Active voice makes your scripts more dynamic and engaging.

- Vary sentence structure: Alternate between short and long sentences to create a more natural flow.

- Use vivid language: Employ descriptive words and imagery to paint a picture in the minds of your viewers.

- Emphasize key points: Repeat important concepts or use pauses to emphasize key takeaways.

Chapter 3 - Day 3 to 6: Course Outline, Content Script Writing with Visual Cues

"The future is AI and education. They are profoundly connected."- Mark Zuckerberg, CEO of Facebook (Meta)

Welcome to Days 4 to 6 of this daily action plan to create a digital course in 14 days. The key tasks in this chapter are:

1. Finalizing the Course Outline using Teachable's AI-Powered Curriculum Outline Generator

2. Writing, editing, and completing the digital course content with visual cues.

We have allocated three days for this chapter because the writing of the course content - topic by topic - with visual cues could be a time-intensive process.

It is important to have a highly organized system of preparing, numbering, and storing your visual cues or aids such as images, screenshots of spreadsheets or documents, or PowerPoint

slides. On the course content script, there will be an indication or notation of the numbered visual cue that relates to the lesson point that is being presented.

This process of adding visual cues to the course scripts will be crucial in streamlining the video creation downstream.

Step-by-Step Guide for Using Teachable's AI Curriculum Outline Generator

Step 1: Accessing the Tool in Teachable

- Log In to Teachable: Start by logging into your Teachable account.

- Navigate to Your Course: Go to the course creation area or select the course you want to work on if it's already created.

Step 2: Starting the AI Curriculum Generator

- Find the Curriculum Generator: Look for the option to use the AI-powered curriculum generator. This might be located in the course setup or curriculum section.

- Initiate the Generator: Click on the button or link to start the curriculum generation process.

Step 3: Inputting Course Information

- Course Description: Input a brief but comprehensive description of your photography course. For example: "This course provides an in-depth look into basic photography skills, covering topics like aperture, shutter speed, ISO, composition, and lighting. It's designed for beginners who want to understand the fundamentals of photography and learn how to take better photos."

- Specific Topics (if prompted): You might be asked to input specific topics you want to cover. List them out, such as "Understanding Aperture," "Mastering Shutter Speed," "ISO and Exposure," etc.

Step 4: Generating the Outline

- Run the Generator: After inputting your course information, click the button to generate the curriculum outline.

- Wait for the Process to Complete: The AI will analyze your input and create a structured outline.

Step 5: Reviewing and Customizing the Outline

- Review the Generated Outline: Look over the sections, modules, and lesson titles that the AI has created.

- Make Adjustments: You can rearrange, add, or delete parts of the outline. For example, you might want to add a specific module on "Choosing the Right Camera" or rearrange the order of topics.

Step 6: Finalizing Your Curriculum

- Refine and Detail Each Section: Add specific details or notes to each section or lesson based on what you plan to cover.

- Integrate with Course Content: Start creating detailed content or scripts for each part of the AI-generated outline.

Example of Curriculum Outline Using Teachable's AI Curriculum Outline Generator

Short Course on Photography

Introduction to Photography: Basics of Photography, Importance of Understanding Your Camera.

Module 1: Understanding Your Camera:
- Lesson 1: Aperture and Depth of Field
- Lesson 2: Shutter Speed and Motion
- Lesson 3: ISO and Light Sensitivity

Module 2: Composition and Framing:
- Lesson 1: Rule of Thirds
- Lesson 2: Leading Lines
- Lesson 3: Use of Color and Contrast

Module 3: Lighting Techniques:
- Lesson 1: Natural vs. Artificial Light
- Lesson 2: The Golden Hour
- Lesson 3: Shadows and Silhouettes

This structured approach allows you to create a well-organized and comprehensive course outline using Teachable's AI tool, ensuring that your course subject covers all the essential topics in a logical and pedagogically sound sequence.

Factors Influencing Script Writing Time

Course Complexity and Length:

Longer and more complex courses naturally take more time to script. Each topic needs to be explained clearly, and corresponding visuals need to be identified and described.

Research and Content Accuracy:

Time spent researching to ensure the accuracy and relevance of your content will add to the scriptwriting process.

Experience in Scriptwriting:

If you're experienced in writing scripts, especially for educational content, you might be faster. For beginners, there might be a learning curve.
Quality of Visuals and Integration:

The process of deciding which visuals to use and where to place them in your script can be time-consuming, especially if you aim for high-quality, engaging content.

Estimating Script Writing Time

2-3 Days Estimate: For a moderately sized course, allocating 2 to 3 days for scriptwriting with visual cues is reasonable. This allows you time to carefully think through each section, research as needed, and plan the visuals effectively.

Day-by-Day Breakdown:

- Day 1: Focus on outlining the entire course and writing a rough draft for a portion of it. Decide on the main visuals you will need.

- Day 2: Continue with detailed scriptwriting, refining what was written on Day 1 and planning the integration of visuals.

- Day 3: Finish the script, review it for coherence and flow, and finalize the visual cues.

Scriptwriting a Digital Course with Visual Cues

1. Preliminary Planning

- Outline Your Course Content: Define the major topics and subtopics of your course.

- Identify Key Visuals: Determine what types of visuals (diagrams, screenshots, slides, etc.) will be needed for each section.

2. Scriptwriting with Visual Cues

- Start Writing the Script: Begin with an introduction and proceed to write the script for each section.

- Incorporate Visual Cues: As you write, insert cues for where visuals should be included. For instance, "[Insert Image: Camera Parts Diagram, Ref: V01]".

3. Organizing and Referencing Visuals

- Numbering System: Assign a unique reference number or code to each visual. For example, "V01" for the first visual, "V02" for the second, and so on.

- Visual Asset Folder: Create a digital folder to store all your visual assets. Organize the folder with subfolders named according to the sections of your course.

4. Detailed Description of Visuals

- Describe Each Visual: In your script, provide a brief description of what each visual will depict or convey. This is especially useful if you are not the one creating the visuals.

5. Matching Script with Visuals

- Catalog of Visuals: Create a catalog or spreadsheet that lists all visuals with their reference numbers, descriptions, and file names.

- Easy Retrieval: Ensure each visual in your digital folder matches its reference number and description in the catalog.

6. Review and Adjustments

- Script Review: Go through the script to ensure that visual cues are correctly placed, and the descriptions match what you intend to show.

- Adjust as Needed: If a particular section of the script seems to need more visual aid, adjust your script and visual references accordingly.

7. Finalizing the Script

- Consistency Check: Make sure the reference system is consistently applied throughout the script.

- Final Review: Ensure that the script flows smoothly and that the integration of visuals will be logical and beneficial for learners.

Example: Script with Visuals for a Short Course on Photography

Sample Visual Cue in Script: "Understanding Aperture: [Insert Image: Aperture Settings, Ref: V03]. The aperture controls the amount of light that enters the lens..."

Visual Asset Folder: A folder titled "Photography Course" with subfolders like "Aperture," "Shutter Speed," etc.

Catalog/Spreadsheet: A document listing V03 - Aperture Settings, aperture_settings.jpg, located in the Aperture folder.

Tips for Effective Script Writing with Visual Cues

- Use a Clear and Consistent Labeling System: Consistency in labeling visuals makes it easier to match them with their cues in the script.

- Maintain a Visual Asset List: Keeping a detailed list or spreadsheet helps in tracking and updating your visual assets.

- Regularly Sync Script and Visuals: Periodically check to ensure that your visuals are in sync with the script cues.

By following these steps, you create a well-structured script with effective visual integration, making the course engaging and easier to understand for learners. The systematic approach to organizing visuals also streamlines the process of video production, ensuring a smooth workflow.

Overall Impact
While script writing with visual cues is more time-consuming, it ultimately leads to a more streamlined and efficient video creation process. The initial time investment in scriptwriting pays off by making the subsequent stages more straightforward and less prone to errors or extensive reworking.

This approach ensures that your course videos are not only informative but also visually engaging and well-structured, which is key to maintaining student interest and facilitating learning.

In summary, the extra effort in scriptwriting, when balanced with good organization and preparation of visuals, makes the video creation process more manageable and can significantly enhance the quality of your final course content.

Editing the Completed Course Lesson or Script with Grammarly

To be more efficient and depending on the segment course topic file size, we suggest uploading up to 4 MB (megabytes) of combined files at a time with Grammarly. Grammarly can accept up to 4 MB of document file size for each upload.

1. **Initial Review:** Run your completed scripts through Grammarly to check for grammatical errors, typos, readability issues, and plagiarism.

2. **Refinements:** Make the necessary corrections suggested by Grammarly. Pay special attention to clarity and conciseness.

Fine-tuning the script for TTS conversion

3. **Adapting for Spoken Language:** Modify the script to suit spoken language. This may involve simplifying sentences and ensuring a conversational tone.

4. **TTS-Friendly Formatting:** Structure your script in short paragraphs and include cues for intonation and

pauses, making it easier for the TTS tool to produce natural-sounding audio.

Importance Of Segmenting The Curriculum Scripts Topic-By-Topic (Or Chapter-By-Chapter) To Prepare The Scripts Correctly For TTS Conversion

This method offers several benefits:

1. **Segmented Learning:** By dividing the course into distinct chapters or topics, learners can absorb information in manageable portions, enhancing understanding and retention.

2. **Focused Attention:** Each audio segment focuses on a single topic, which helps maintain the learner's attention and interest.

3. **Convenience for Pausing and Resuming:** After each chapter, instructing learners to pause for a quiz and then resume with the next chapter makes the learning process interactive and self-paced. This is

particularly effective for online learning, where learners have control over their pace.

4. **Enhanced Engagement:** Breaking the course into chapters with quizzes at the end of each keeps learners engaged. It provides a clear structure and goals for each learning session.

5. **Flexibility in Course Navigation:** Learners have the flexibility to revisit specific chapters for review without having to search through a long, continuous audio file.

6. **Ease of Production:** From a video production standpoint, converting audio chapter by chapter allows you to focus on smaller sections of content at a time, making the process more manageable and less prone to errors.

Implementation Example

1. **End of Chapter Audio Cue:** At the end of each audio chapter, include a statement like, "Now,

please pause this video and complete the Quiz to test your understanding of [topic]. When you're ready, proceed to the next chapter."

2. **Next Chapter Start:** The beginning of each new chapter can start with a brief recap or an introduction to the new topic to smoothly transition learners from one section to the next.

4

Chapter 4 - Days 7 to 8: Proficiency with Speechify and TTS Audio Conversion

"With AI, personalized learning can become a reality, addressing the unique needs of each student." Sal Khan, Founder of Khan Academy:

Welcome to Day 7 of our 14-day action plan to create

a complete digital course using Teachable as our online course platform. Our game plan for today is to do a segmented topic-by-topic TTS conversion of course scripts, which have been similarly segmented until all topics have been converted.

At its core, TTS is a form of speech synthesis that converts written text into spoken words, using artificial intelligence and natural language processing.

This technology mimics human speech, allowing for the creation of audio content without the need for traditional voice recording. The beauty of TTS lies in its ability to produce clear, natural-sounding voices across various languages and accents, making it a versatile tool for global content creators.

Speechify, our recommended AI-powered TTS tool,
leverages this technology, offering an intuitive platform
where users can input their scripts and transform them into
high-quality audio. The AI behind Speechify analyzes the
text for proper pronunciation, intonation, and emotion,
ensuring the output is not just accurate but also engaging
for the listener. This makes Speechify an invaluable tool on
Day 4 of the written script-to-audio conversion process,
where the focus is entirely on converting topic-by-topic

well-crafted scripts into captivating audio narratives, ready to be paired with visuals in subsequent steps.

Why Speechify?

There are other TTS AI-powered tools out there, and you might already be using one. For the complete beginner, we recommend Speechify for short-form audio content due to its ability to convert text into natural-sounding speech, eliminating the need for voice recording. Because we are doing TTS conversion topic by topic, we are essentially doing short-form audio content.

The advent of AI TTS tools like Speechify is particularly beneficial for creators who prefer to remain anonymous or lack recording equipment. Speechify offers a range of realistic and engaging voices, adding a professional touch to the audio component of the videos. Its ease of use and high-quality output make it an excellent tool for efficiently producing short-form content, ensuring that the videos are both engaging and accessible to a wide audience.

Chapter 4 - the first part of Day 7 will be devoted to building your proficiency with Speechify. As you explore Speechify, follow the guideposts below for a structured learning discovery and practice.

- Deep Dive into Speechify Features: Explore the range of voices, languages, and customization options available in Speechify.

- Script Preparation: Refine your script, ensuring it's ready for conversion to speech.

- Text-to-Speech Conversion:

- Audio Customization:

- Quality Check:

- Revisions if Needed:

- Finalizing the Audio File:

Speechify TTS is relatively straightforward to use.

1. Users typically need to get accustomed to selecting voices, adjusting speech speed, and converting text to speech.
2. The interface is user-friendly, and most find it easy to navigate after a few tries.

Here are Your Practice Examples.

- **Blog Post Narration:** Take a blog post and convert it into an audio file using Speechify. Pay attention to adjusting the voice and speed to match the tone of the post.

- **News Article Reading:** Convert a recent news article into a speech. This will help you get used to pronouncing different types of words and names correctly.

- **Your Own Written Script:** Use a script you've written, perhaps a short story or introduction, and convert it into speech. This will give you a feel for how your own written content sounds when narrated.

TTS Conversion of Segmented Course Scripts and Completing the Audio Script Preparation And Refinement *(for video conversion as the next step)*

The 2nd part of Day 7 is the actual conversion to audio of the segmented topic-by-topic course scripts. Here are the steps to follow:

1. Text-to-Speech Conversion with Speechify:

Script Preparation: Before inputting the script into Speechify, ensure it is segmented topic by topic and formatted for spoken language. This includes using conversational tones, short sentences, and clear paragraph breaks.

Conversion Process:

- Upload or copy-paste the script into Speechify.

- Choose a voice that aligns with your course's tone and audience. Speechify offers a variety of voices, so select one that best fits the style of your content.

- Convert the text to audio. Pay attention to how Speechify interprets punctuation and formatting, as this can affect the flow of speech.

2. Audio Customization and Adjustment:

Voice and Pace: Experiment with different voice options and playback speeds. The pace should be comfortable for learning, not too fast to overwhelm, nor too slow to bore.

Tone Adjustments: Adjust the tone to suit the content. For example, a more upbeat tone might be suitable for motivational content, while a calm, steady voice might be better for complex, technical topics.

3. Quality Check and Revisions:

Listening and Reviewing: Listen to the audio files in their entirety. Pay attention to pronunciation, clarity, and natural flow.

Making Revisions: If certain sections sound awkward or unclear, adjust the script and redo the TTS conversion. Sometimes, simple rephrasing can significantly improve the audio quality.

4. Finalizing the Audio File:

Editing: If you have audio editing software, use it to make fine adjustments, like removing unnecessary pauses or adding slight pauses for emphasis.

File Saving: Save or export the audio in a format suitable for your course platform. Ensure each audio file is correctly named and corresponds to its course segment.

Additional Considerations:

- Accessibility: Consider how your TTS audio will work in conjunction with on-screen visuals or text for students who might have different learning preferences.

- Backup Your Scripts: Keep both the original and edited scripts saved, as they might be useful for future courses or updates.

- By adding these details, your TTS process becomes more comprehensive, catering to various aspects of converting written course material into engaging and effective audio content.

The detailed steps above help make the TTS conversion of written course material into engaging and effective audio content.

Chapter 5 - Days 9 to 11:
Digital Course Video Production

"AI is going to change the workplace, and that includes how we learn and teach."

- Sheryl Sandberg, COO of Facebook (Meta)

The video creation industry is undergoing a significant

transformation, largely driven by advancements in AI-
powered video conversion technology. This innovative
approach is democratizing video production by making it
accessible and achievable for a broader range of
individuals, regardless of their technical expertise.

AI-driven platforms interpret and transform text-based
content into visual narratives, automating the process of
syncing scripts with appropriate visuals, animations, and
music. This shift is not just about simplifying video
production; it's about leveling the playing field, allowing
anyone with a creative vision to produce captivating and
professional-looking videos, thus expanding the creative
landscape and fostering diverse content creation.

AI-powered video conversion tools are revolutionizing the
field of video production by making it accessible to a wider
audience. This technology uses artificial intelligence to
transform text-based content into engaging video formats.

By analyzing the script, AI identifies key elements and themes, suggesting relevant visuals and animations to create a cohesive and compelling video. This process significantly reduces the time and expertise traditionally required in video editing, opening the doors for creators of all skill levels to produce professional-quality videos.

Why Lumen5?

There are other video conversion AI-powered tools out there, and you might already be using one. For the complete beginner, we recommend Lumen5 for short-form faceless digital course audio-to-video conversion. Since we are segmenting the course audio topic by topic, the resulting video will also be topic by topic and essentially short-form.

Lumen5, in particular, stands at the forefront of this revolution in AI-powered video creation. It simplifies video creation by automating the process of matching text content with appropriate imagery and layouts. Users can input their script or content, and Lumen5's AI algorithms will suggest a storyboard, visuals, and even background music.

This approach not only streamlines video production but also ensures a high standard of quality and relevance, making it an indispensable tool for creators aiming to engage and expand their audience.

Deep Dive Into Lumen5

As you step into Chapter 5: "Digital Course Video Production," prepare to transform your carefully crafted and segmented scripts into actual videos.

This chapter is your introduction to the world of Lumen5, an intuitive, AI-powered video creation platform that simplifies the process of producing short-form content. You will learn how to navigate its user-friendly interface, seamlessly integrating Speechify's audio narrations with your chosen visuals. This chapter demystifies the art of video editing, making it accessible even to those with no prior experience.

Here, we'll also delve into the creative aspects of video editing, exploring how to use transitions and effects to add a professional touch to your videos. These enhancements are more than just aesthetic choices; they play a crucial role in keeping your audience engaged. By the end of this chapter, you'll have the skills to create videos that not only tell a story but do so in a visually captivating manner, setting the stage for more advanced techniques in the next chapter.

Let us zero in on Lumen5's features and capabilities:

- **Inputting the Script:** Learn how to input your Speechify audio script into Lumen5.

- **Exploring AI Recommendations:** Understand how Lumen5 suggests visuals and layouts based on your script.

- **Selecting Visuals and Themes:** Begin selecting and customizing visuals and themes for your video.

- **Starting the Video Assembly:** Start the process of assembling your video aligning visuals with the audio narrative.

- Basic Editing Techniques: Learn and apply basic editing techniques in Lumen5.

- Saving Progress: Understand how to save your work in progress on Lumen5.

This day is dedicated to harnessing Lumen5's AI capabilities to start transforming your digital course audio content into a visually engaging video, setting the foundation for more advanced editing in the following days.

Here Are The Start-To-Finish Exercise Examples For Getting Proficient With Lumen5 In One Day:

Create a Short News Recap Video:

Find a recent news article.

- Summarize the main points in a short script.

- Use Lumen5 to create a video that highlights these points with relevant stock images and video clips.

- Add background music and a concluding slide.

Make a Promotional Video for an Imaginary Product:

Invent a product or service.

- Write a brief script that describes its features and benefits.

- Use Lumen5 to visually bring these features to life, using images, text overlays, and a persuasive voiceover or music track.

Develop a How-To or Tutorial Video:

- Choose a simple topic, like a basic recipe or a craft project.

- Write a step-by-step guide.

- Create a video in Lumen5 using this guide, adding relevant visuals and text to clearly illustrate each step.

These exercises cover a range of video types and will help you explore and understand the various features of Lumen5.

Creating A Digital Course Video With Lumen5 From Start To Finish Involves Several Key Steps:

- **Sign In and Start a New Project:** Log into your Lumen5 account and click on 'Create a Video' to start a new project.

- **Choose a Template or Start from Scratch:** Select from various templates that suit your video style, or start with a blank canvas.

- **Add Your Script:** You can either manually enter your script or upload a document. Lumen5 will automatically suggest relevant media based on the text.

- **Select Media:** Browse through Lumen5's library of stock photos and videos, or upload your own. Drag and drop these into your video timeline.

- **Edit Text and Timing:** Adjust the text overlays on each scene for clarity and impact. Ensure the timing aligns well with the narrative flow of your video.

- **Customize with Branding:** Add your brand colors, logos, and other custom elements to maintain consistency with your branding.

- **Add Music and Voiceover:** Choose from Lumen5's library of royalty-free music or upload your own track. You can also add a voiceover.

- **Preview and Edit:** Watch the preview of your video, making any necessary edits to improve flow, visual appeal, or narrative impact.

- **Render and Export:** Once you're satisfied with the video, render it. After rendering, you can download the video file or directly share it on social media platforms.

- **Review and Adjust as Needed:** After exporting, you may want to review the video again and make any final adjustments before using it for your intended purpose.

This process in Lumen5 is designed to be intuitive and user-friendly, even for those with little to no video editing experience.

The Value Of Augmenting Your Learning Tools By Watching Lumen5 Beginner Tutorials On YouTube

Watching beginner YouTube tutorials on Lumen5 can be incredibly valuable, especially if you find yourself stuck or confused by written instructions. These tutorials offer visual and practical demonstrations that can make complex processes clearer and easier to understand.

They often cover a range of topics, from basic navigation to advanced features, providing insights that might not be immediately apparent from written guides alone. Additionally, seeing someone else use the tool can provide new ideas and approaches to video creation that can enhance your learning experience and proficiency with Lumen5.

Using Lumen5 for Slide-Based Digital Courses

Prepare Your Slides/Screenshots:

- Before you start with Lumen5, prepare the slides or screenshots you want to use in your course. These could be images of PowerPoint slides, screenshots of software interfaces, diagrams, or any other visual elements crucial for your lesson.

- Ensure that these images are clear and high-quality to be easily readable and understandable when displayed in your course video.

Creating a New Video Project in Lumen5:

- Log into your Lumen5 account and start a new video project.

- Choose the format that best fits your course's platform (e.g., standard, square, or vertical).

Uploading Your Slides/Screenshots:

- In the Lumen5 interface, go to the 'Media' section, where you can upload your own images.

- Upload the prepared slides or screenshots here. Lumen5 allows you to import these images into your video project.

Adding Images to Your Video:

- Drag and drop your uploaded slides/screenshots onto the timeline where you want them to appear in your video.

- Adjust the duration for which each slide should be

displayed. For teaching purposes, you might want to keep each slide on the screen longer than the default duration to give students enough time to understand the content.

Adding Narration or Text:

- If you have a voiceover, you can sync your slides with the audio for each segment of your lesson.

- Alternatively, you can use Lumen5's text overlay feature to add key points or explanations that correspond with each slide.

Fine-Tuning and Transitions:

- Use Lumen5's editing tools to fine-tune the appearance of each slide in the video. This can include adding transitions, adjusting alignment, or modifying the background.

- Ensure that the transitions between slides are smooth and maintain the flow of the lesson.

Preview and Export:

- Once your video is assembled, preview it to ensure that all slides are displayed correctly, and the narration (if any) is properly synchronized.

- Export your final video and upload it to your course platform.

Additional Tips

- Consistency: Maintain a consistent style throughout your video to make it visually coherent and professional.

- Accessibility: Consider adding captions or subtitles, especially if you're using voice narration, to make your content accessible to a wider audience.

- Testing: Before finalizing, test your video with a small group of users to gather feedback on its effectiveness and clarity.

By following these steps, you can leverage Lumen5 to create slide-based educational videos that focus on one concept at a time, ensuring that your students remain engaged and absorb the material effectively.

Chapter 6 - Day 12: Quiz Creation and Integration

"AI is changing the way we access and process information, including educational content." - Susan Wojcicki, CEO of YouTube.

As we embark on Chapter 6 of our comprehensive

guide to creating a digital course, we delve into the pivotal realm of Quiz Creation and Integration, a process crucial for reinforcing learning and enhancing student engagement. Over the next two days, we will harness the innovative capabilities of Teachable's AI-powered quiz generator, a tool designed to streamline the quiz creation process, making it both efficient and effective.

This chapter is dedicated to guiding you through the seamless integration of interactive quizzes into your course, ensuring they align perfectly with your instructional content and learning objectives.

Simplifying a Time-Consuming Task

The beauty of Teachable's quiz generator lies in its ability to simplify what was once a time-consuming task. By leveraging AI technology, the tool intuitively generates quiz questions that are tailored to the content of your lessons, providing an automated yet personalized approach to assessment. This chapter will walk you through the nuances of utilizing this tool, from selecting the appropriate sections of your course for quiz placement to customizing the automatically generated questions to fit your unique course style and needs.

Furthermore, we recognize the importance of quizzes in not only assessing student comprehension but also in providing valuable Feedback to learners. Thus, our focus will also extend to the strategic integration of these quizzes within your course structure. We aim to ensure that each Quiz serves as a natural extension of the learning journey, enhancing the overall educational experience.

By the end of this chapter, you will be equipped with the knowledge and skills to seamlessly weave engaging and informative quizzes into your course, elevating the interactive dimension of your digital teaching endeavor.

Generating Quizzes Using Teachable's AI-Powered Tool

1. Accessing the Quiz Generator

- Log In to Teachable: Start by logging into your Teachable account.

- Navigate to Your Course: Select the course where you want to add the Quiz.

2. Opening the Curriculum Section

- Go to the Curriculum Tab: In your course's dashboard, find and open the "Curriculum" tab where you manage your course content.

3. Selecting the Lesson for the Quiz

- Choose the Appropriate Lesson: Identify the lesson after which you want to insert the Quiz. The AI tool will use the content of this lesson to generate relevant quiz questions.

4. Starting the Quiz Generation

- Initiate the Quiz Generator: Look for the option to create a quiz, often labeled as "Add Quiz" or a similar term.
- Use AI Features: If Teachable offers an AI-powered option, select it to automate the creation of quiz questions based on the chosen lesson's content.

5. Customizing the Quiz

- Review AI-Generated Questions: The tool will provide a set of questions. Review these for relevance and accuracy.
- Edit Questions: Modify, add, or remove questions to ensure they meet your course's specific needs and accurately assess students' understanding of the material.

6. Finalizing the Quiz

- Save and Integrate: Once you're satisfied with the Quiz, save it. It will automatically become part of your course's curriculum, positioned after the chosen lesson.

7. Setting Quiz Parameters

- Determine Pass/Fail Criteria: Set the parameters for passing the Quiz, like minimum score requirements.
- Feedback Settings: Decide if and how you want to provide Feedback for each question, such as showing correct answers after submission.

Understanding Teachable's User Interface for Quizzes

Standalone Feature: In Teachable, quizzes are a standalone feature that integrates with your course but remains separate from video content. They appear as distinct elements in the course's curriculum flow.

Interactive Interface: Students interact with quizzes directly on the Teachable platform. After completing a video lesson, they can proceed to the Quiz, which is clearly indicated in the course layout.

Navigation Ease: The Teachable interface is intuitive, allowing students to easily find and complete quizzes. They can navigate back and forth between lessons and quizzes as needed.

Quiz Visibility: Quizzes are visible in the course outline and are accessible independently of video content, ensuring that they do not interfere with or disrupt the video learning experience.

By following these steps, you can effectively create and integrate quizzes into your Teachable course, enhancing the learning experience without needing to alter or include them in your video content. This approach leverages Teachable's user-friendly interface and AI capabilities to provide an engaging, interactive, and seamless educational journey for your students.

Visibility of Quiz Answers

Before Taking the Quiz: Generally, the answers to the Quiz are not visible to the learner before taking the Quiz. The purpose of the Quiz is to assess the learner's understanding of the material after they have engaged with the course content.

After Completing the Quiz:

Immediate Feedback: You can set up quizzes in Teachable to provide immediate Feedback. This means that as soon as a learner completes the Quiz, they can see which questions they got right or wrong.

Answer Visibility: You can choose whether to show the correct answers after the Quiz is completed. Some instructors prefer to show the correct answers to enhance learning, while others may choose not to, especially if the Quiz is meant to be a formal assessment.

Timing of Quiz Results

Instant Results: The results of the Quiz, typically in the form of a score or pass/fail status, are usually provided to the learner immediately after they submit their answers. This instant Feedback is part of what makes online learning engaging and effective.

Review Option: Depending on the settings, students may have the option to review the questions along with their answers and the correct answers (if you choose to display them) after completing the Quiz.

Configuring Quizzes in Teachable

Settings: When creating a quiz in Teachable, you have the option to configure these settings. You can decide whether or not to show the correct answers and what kind of Feedback the students receive after completing the Quiz.

Flexibility: Teachable's quiz feature is quite flexible, allowing you to tailor the experience to suit your teaching style and the learning objectives of your course.

Best Practices

Clarify Expectations: It's important to inform students about the quiz format and what kind of Feedback they will receive. This could be mentioned in the course introduction or in the instructions preceding the Quiz.

Use Feedback Effectively: Providing Feedback, whether it includes the correct answers or not, can be a powerful tool for learning. Consider what approach is most beneficial for your students in terms of reinforcing the material and helping them learn from their mistakes.

In summary, Teachable's quizzes are designed to be versatile, giving you control over how and when Quiz answers, and results are shared with learners. This functionality supports a range of teaching approaches and learning experiences within your online course.

Combining Various Elements Into a Cohesive and Functional Online Course

Integration in the context of creating a digital course, particularly on a platform like Teachable, refers to the process of combining various course elements — such as videos, text, quizzes, and other interactive components — into a cohesive and functional online course.

This process ensures that all these different elements work together smoothly to provide a seamless learning experience for the students. Here's how you can achieve this:

Steps for Integration in a Digital Course on Teachable

1. Planning Your Course Structure

- Outline the Course: Define the flow of your course, deciding where each video, reading material, Quiz, or other interactive elements should be placed.

- Sequence of Learning: Arrange the content in a logical order that progressively builds on the learner's knowledge.

2. Uploading and Organizing Content

- Upload Videos: Add your video lectures to the relevant sections of your course. Ensure they are in the format supported by Teachable.

- Add Textual Content: Include readings, PDFs, or textual explanations where necessary.

- Insert Quizzes: Place the quizzes at appropriate points in the course, typically at the end of each major section or lesson.

3. Integrating Interactive Components

- Discussion Forums: If your course includes discussions, set up forums or comment sections for each relevant part of the course.

- External Resources: Link to any external resources or supplementary materials.

4. Ensuring Seamless Navigation

- User-Friendly Design: Organize the course in a way that is easy to navigate. Use clear labels for each section and lesson.

- Test Navigation: Go through the course as a student would to ensure that the transition from one section to another is smooth.

5. Setting Up Course Parameters

- Progress Tracking: Enable features that allow students to track their progress through the course.

- Acccss Scttings: Determine if the course will be self-paced or if content will be released on a schedule.

6. Final Review and Testing

- Review the Course: Go through the entire course to check for any issues – from content errors to technical glitches.

- Test User Experience: Ideally, have a few test users (like colleagues or friends) go through the course to provide feedback on their experience.

7. Making Adjustments

- Incorporate Feedback: Use the Feedback to make necessary adjustments to the course.

- Final Tweaks: Make any last-minute tweaks to optimize the course experience.

8. Launching the Course

- Publish the Course: Once everything is set, publish your course.

- Monitor and Update: After launch, continue to monitor student feedback and engagement, making adjustments where needed.

Summary

Integration is about bringing together all the elements of your digital course in a way that they complement and build upon each other, creating a comprehensive learning experience. This includes not just uploading content but also ensuring that the course is easy to navigate, the elements are logically sequenced, and the overall design supports the learning objectives.

The key is to focus on both the educational content and the user experience to ensure that your course is engaging, informative, and accessible to your students.

7

Chapter 7 - Day 13: Review and Testing

"The AI era is here. It's a tool that will augment our human capabilities."
- Ginni Rometty, Former CEO of IBM:

As we enter Chapter 7 of our comprehensive journey in

digital course creation, we approach a critical phase that
underpins the success and effectiveness of our educational

endeavor – Review and Testing. This chapter is dedicated to the meticulous process of scrutinizing every element of our course, ensuring that the content is not only informative and engaging but also functions seamlessly across different platforms and devices.

The tasks ahead involve a detailed review of our course materials, including videos, quizzes, and interactive components, to identify and rectify any content inaccuracies, technical glitches, or user experience issues.

In this phase, we'll embark on a thorough examination of the course from the learner's perspective, a process pivotal in guaranteeing a smooth and intuitive learning experience. We'll be engaging in a series of rigorous testing protocols, which include soliciting Feedback from a test audience, implementing usability testing strategies, and fine-tuning the course navigation.

Embodying Our Education Vision and Commitment to Quality

This chapter is about refining our course to perfection, ensuring that every aspect, from the clarity of our video lectures to the responsiveness of our interactive quizzes, aligns with the highest standards of online education. By the end of this chapter, our course will not only embody our educational vision but also stand as a testament to our commitment to quality and excellence in digital learning.

Review Process: Start to Finish Steps

- **1. Content Accuracy Review**

  Thoroughly Read and Watch: Go through all text
  and video content to check for accuracy, clarity, and
  relevance.

  Fact-Check: Verify facts, figures, and any technical
  information provided in the course.

- **2. Technical Review**

  Check Video and Audio Quality: Ensure all
  multimedia elements are of high quality, with clear
  audio and visuals.

  Functionality Check: Test all links, downloadable
  materials, and interactive elements for proper
  functionality.

- **3. User Experience Review**

  Navigation: Go through the course as if you were a

student, checking for smooth navigation and logical course flow.

Consistency in Design: Ensure consistency in the layout, fonts, colors, and overall design across the course.

- **4. Accessibility Review**

Compliance with Standards: Check if your course meets accessibility standards, such as providing subtitles for videos and alternative text for images.

- **5. Feedback from Colleagues**

Peer Review: Have colleagues or industry peers review the course and provide Feedback on content and delivery.

- **6. Final Adjustments**

Incorporate Feedback: Make necessary changes based on the reviews and Feedback received.

Testing Process: Start to Finish Steps

- **1. Beta Testing with a Sample Audience**

  Select a Test Group: Invite a small group of users who represent your target audience to take your course.

  Monitor Their Progress: Observe how they interact with the course, noting any confusion or difficulties.

- **2. Collecting and Analyzing Feedback**

  Surveys and Interviews: Use surveys or conduct interviews to gather detailed Feedback from your test group.

  Identify Common Issues: Look for patterns in the Feedback that indicate areas needing improvement.

- **3. Usability Testing**

  Task Completion: Ask testers to complete specific tasks and observe how easily they can navigate and understand the course.

  Ease of Use Assessment: Evaluate the overall user experience, focusing on how intuitive and user-friendly the course is.

- **4. Technical Stress Test**

Load Testing: If possible, test how the course performs under heavy load conditions.

Compatibility Check: Ensure the course works well across different devices and browsers.

- **5. Implementing Changes**

Refine Based on Testing: Use the insights gained from testing to make improvements to the course.

Retest if Necessary: If significant changes are made, consider a second round of testing to ensure all issues are resolved.

- **6. Final Review**

Final Run-Through: Go through the entire course one last time to ensure all changes have been implemented effectively.

Sign-Off: Once satisfied, give your final approval for the course to go live.

By following these structured steps in both reviewing and testing your course, you can ensure that it not only meets your educational objectives but also provides an engaging, accessible, and seamless experience for your learners.

Chapter 8 - Day 14: Final Adjustments and Lessons Learned

"AI-powered tools can help us to create more immersive learning experiences that will help students to learn more effectively." - Geoffrey Hinton is a Canadian-British computer scientist and co-director of the Canadian Institute for Advanced Research.

In Chapter 8, the penultimate stage of our digital course

creation journey, we focus on the crucial task of making Final Adjustments. This phase is all about refining and polishing every aspect of our course to ensure it's ready for a successful launch. It's a critical step where we take a step back to review our course in its entirety, fine-tuning the details and making sure everything aligns perfectly with our educational goals and standards. The final adjustments are not just about correcting errors but also about enhancing the overall quality of the course, ensuring that it delivers a compelling and enriching learning experience.

A Keen Eye for Detail

This chapter guides us through a meticulous process of revision and enhancement. We'll scrutinize every module, every lesson, and every interactive element, making sure that they collectively form a coherent and engaging learning pathway. From smoothing out any rough

edges in our video content to ensuring the quizzes accurately assess and reinforce learning, this stage is our last opportunity to perfect our course before it goes live. The process demands a keen eye for detail and a commitment to excellence, ensuring that what we offer to our learners is nothing short of the best.

Start to Finish Steps for Final Adjustments

- **1. Comprehensive Course Review**

  Review All Content: Go through every piece of content again, including videos, texts, quizzes, and additional resources, looking for areas that might need refinement.

  Focus on Details: Pay attention to details like grammar, spelling, graphical consistency, and alignment of multimedia elements.

- **2. Feedback Incorporation**

  Gather All Feedback: Compile all the Feedback received from your beta testers, colleagues, and any other reviews.

  Prioritize Adjustments: Identify the most critical Feedback and prioritize the adjustments that need to be made.

- **3. Revisiting Course Objectives**

  Alignment with Goals: Ensure that your course content and structure align with the initial learning objectives and course goals.

Relevance and Accuracy: Double-check the relevance and accuracy of all the information provided in the course.

- **4. Technical Fine-Tuning**

Enhance Video and Audio Quality: Make any necessary improvements to the video and audio quality.

Interactive Elements: Ensure all interactive elements, like quizzes and discussion forums, are functioning correctly.

- **5. User Experience Optimization**

Improve Navigation: Make sure the course navigation is intuitive and user-friendly.

Consistency Check: Ensure consistency in design, language, and presentation throughout the course.

- **6. Final Accessibility Check**

Accessibility Standards: Verify that the course meets essential accessibility standards, such as subtitles for videos and alt text for images.

- **7. Last Round of Testing**

Final Testing: Conduct a final round of testing, ideally with a few members of your target audience, to ensure all adjustments are effective.

- **8. Course Closure**

Final Approval: Give your course final approval before declaring it ready for launch.

Prepare for Launch: Start preparing for the course launch, including marketing and student enrollment strategies.

By meticulously following these steps for final adjustments, you ensure that your course is not only free of errors but also polished to a high standard. This phase is crucial in transforming a good course into a great one, making it ready to provide an exceptional learning experience to your students.

Lessons Learned: The Value of Retrospectives

As we conclude our 14-day action plan for creating a digital course, it's crucial to pause and reflect on the journey we've embarked upon. The "Lessons Learned and the Value of Retrospectives" section is dedicated to this introspection and knowledge capture. This phase is not merely about listing what went right or wrong; it's a deeper dive into the experiences, insights, and realizations we gained throughout the process.

Capturing these lessons while they are fresh in our minds is pivotal. It's about understanding the nuances that led to success, the hurdles that taught us resilience, and the streamlining strategies that enhanced our efficiency.

Gems of Wisdom

These lessons, often subtle and nuanced, are the gems of wisdom that can profoundly impact our future endeavors in digital course creation.

Structure for Lessons Learned

1. **Reflecting on the Process:**

   Encourage a thorough reflection on each stage of the course creation process.

Discuss both the successes and challenges encountered.

2. **Documenting Key Learnings:**

   Create a systematic approach to document insights, including what worked well and what could be improved.

   Emphasize the importance of writing these down immediately to avoid losing valuable insights.

3. **Analyzing Mistakes and Successes:**

   Encourage an honest analysis of mistakes made and what was learned from them.

   Highlight the successes and what contributed to these positive outcomes.

4. **Streamlining Future Workflows:**

   Identify any streamlining steps or efficiencies discovered that could benefit future courses.

   Discuss how these can be integrated into future workflows.

5. **Capturing Unexpected Insights:**

   Encourage noting down any unexpected insights or creative ideas that emerged during the process.

   Discuss how these can be leveraged in future projects.

6. **Creating a Knowledge Base:**

   Suggest compiling these learnings into a knowledge base for future reference.

   Highlight how this can serve as a valuable resource for ongoing improvement and innovation.

7. **Sharing and Collaboration:**

   Encourage sharing these learnings with team members or peers.

   Discuss how collaborative reflection can lead to a richer understanding and more comprehensive improvements.

8. **Applying Learnings to Future Projects:**

   Discuss strategies for applying these lessons to future digital course projects.

   Emphasize the iterative nature of learning and improving in the realm of digital education.

By dedicating time to this reflective practice, you not only enhance your own skill set and knowledge but also contribute to a culture of continuous learning and improvement. This section will be instrumental in shaping more streamlined, effective, and successful digital course projects in the future.

Closing Summary

As we draw the curtain on this transformative journey, it's essential to take a moment to reflect on the remarkable transition you've undergone. Starting as a total beginner, you have now emerged as a skilled creator of faceless digital courses, equipped with a comprehensive toolkit of skills and knowledge.

From Novice to Expert

This journey has been about more than just learning the mechanics of course creation; it's been about cultivating a mindset of innovation, creativity, and continuous learning. You've navigated through the complexities of scripting with visual cues, mastering AI-powered tools, and synthesizing diverse elements into cohesive, engaging online courses. Your journey exemplifies a significant metamorphosis from novice to expert, laying a solid foundation for your ongoing development in the world of digital education.

Dynamic Not Static

The skills and insights you've gained are not static; they're dynamic and will continue to evolve with each course you create. The beauty of this process lies in its iterative nature — each course you develop will be an opportunity to refine your techniques, discover more efficient workflows, and enhance the quality of your content. Remember, the journey of learning and improvement never truly ends.

Within a mere 30 days, you have the potential to produce not just one but two comprehensive courses. Imagine the possibilities that unfold over two months, four months, a year. Your trajectory is only limited by the boundaries of your imagination and commitment.

The estimated time of 14 days to complete one faceless digital video course suitable to be uploaded to an online course platform was calibrated for beginners doing it for the first time. As they create more digital courses, their proficiency and expertise will mushroom, and they will likely find ways to streamline and shorten the 14-day start-to-finish original estimate.

No Time To Waste

Now, with the knowledge and experience in hand, there is no time to waste. The digital learning landscape is rapidly expanding, and your contribution to it is eagerly awaited. Embrace the iterative nature of this craft; with each course, you will uncover shortcuts and strategies that expedite the process without compromising on quality.

Your journey is a testament to the fact that with dedication, the right tools, and a willingness to learn, transformation is not just possible but inevitable. Step forward with confidence, knowing that each course you create is not just an educational product but a stepping stone in your continual path of professional and personal growth in the exciting realm of digital education.

Send for your FREE Bonus Gift: *A PDF Document on "How to Promote and Monetize Your Faceless Digital Course Videos."*

We have prepared a PDF document about the different traditional and non-traditional ways you can market, promote, and, yes, monetize your faceless digital course videos.

While it is not part of the coverage of this book, we would be delighted to send it to you as a way of saying **"thank you"** for purchasing this book. We hope that the book is informative and useful and deserving of your stellar review.

Below is the link to sign up for the *PDF Document to Market and Monetize Your Digital Course Videos*

https://forms.gle/P2StV15DR23ZgH
MB8

You may also email the author and ask for this FREE
GIFT:

simonelee0822@gmail.com

Glossary of Terms

Accessibility Features: Elements such as captions or descriptive audio that make videos accessible to a wider audience, including those with disabilities.

Adaptive Learning: A technology-driven approach to e-learning that personalizes the learning experience based on the learner's performance and preferences.

Affiliate Marketing: A marketing arrangement where an online retailer pays a commission to an external website for traffic or sales generated from its referrals.

AI (Artificial Intelligence): A branch of computer science dealing with the simulation of intelligent behavior in computers.

Algorithm: A set of rules or processes used in calculations or problem-solving operations, especially by a computer. In digital marketing, it refers to the logic used by platforms to determine content display.

Analytics: The discovery, interpretation, and communication of meaningful patterns in data, particularly valuable in understanding audience behavior in e-learning and digital marketing.

Aspect Ratio: The proportional relationship between a video's width and height.

Audience Segmentation: The process of dividing an audience into smaller groups with similar characteristics. Useful in both topic selection and digital marketing.

B-Roll: Supplementary footage that can be included in your videos, often providing context or visual interest.

Bitrate: The rate at which video data is processed, measured in bits per second (bps). Higher bitrates generally mean better video quality.

Call to Action (CTA): A statement or button in a video that encourages viewers to take a specific action, such as subscribing or visiting a website.

Chatbot: An AI-powered tool used for simulating conversations with human users, especially on websites.

Click-Through Rate (CTR): A metric that measures how often viewers click on a link or call to action in a video.

Compression: The process of reducing the size of a video file, which can affect its quality.

Content Curation: The process of gathering information relevant to a particular topic or area of interest for inclusion in a video or course.

Content Management System (CMS): Software that helps users create, manage, and modify content on a website without the need for specialized technical knowledge.

Content Strategy: The planning, development, and management of content—written or in other media. Crucial for topic selection and course structuring.

Conversion Funnel: A model describing the various stages a customer goes through before making a purchase decision.

Conversion Rate: The percentage of viewers who take a desired action (e.g., signing up for a course) after watching a video.

Copywriting: The act of writing text for the purpose of advertising or other forms of marketing relevant to scriptwriting and course promotion.

Course Analytics: Data that provides insights into the performance and engagement of an online course.

Course Module: A distinct section or part of a digital course focusing on a specific topic.

Digital Storytelling: The practice of using digital tools to tell a story, often used in video production.

E-Learning: Learning is conducted via electronic media, typically on the Internet.

Engagement Metrics: Data points that measure how viewers interact with a video, including likes, shares, comments, and watch time.

Engagement Rate: A metric that measures the level of audience interaction with your video content.

Engagement Strategies: Techniques used to maintain and increase the interaction of learners with the course content.

Feedback Mechanisms: Tools and methods used to gather

Feedback from learners essential for course improvement.

Frame Rate (FPS): The frequency at which consecutive images (frames) appear in a video, measured in frames per second.

Gamification: The application of game-design elements and principles in non-game contexts, such as e-learning, to enhance user engagement and learning.

Grammarly: An AI writing assistant used for grammar checking, spell checking, and plagiarism detection.

Green Screen: A technique for changing the background in a video by replacing a solid-colored background with a different image or video.

Infographic: A visual representation of information or data, often included in educational videos for clarity.

Instructional Design: The practice of creating instructional experiences that make the acquisition of knowledge and skill more efficient and effective a core concept in e-learning course development.

Interactive Elements in E-Learning: Components like quizzes, polls, and interactive discussions that engage learners actively.

Interactive Video: A type of video that allows viewer interaction, such as clicking on elements within the video.

Jasper: An AI-powered content generation tool used for scriptwriting and idea generation.

Keyword Optimization: The process of researching, analyzing, and selecting the best keywords to drive traffic from search engines to your website or online content.

Lead Generation: The initiation of consumer interest or inquiry into products or services of a business, often a key goal in digital marketing.

Learning Management System (LMS): Software used for delivering, tracking, and managing training/education courses.

Learning Objectives: Specific goals that learners are expected to achieve by the end of the course module or course.

Lumen5: An AI-powered video creation tool that transforms text content into engaging video formats.

Machine Learning: A type of AI that allows software applications to become more accurate at predicting outcomes without being explicitly programmed to do so.

Marketing Funnels in E-Learning: A model describing the stages a potential learner goes through, from becoming aware of a course to enrolling.

Metadata: Additional information about a video, including titles, tags, and descriptions, which help with search engine optimization.

Microlearning: An e-learning strategy that involves delivering content in small, specific bursts, focusing on key topics or skills.

Mobile Learning (M-Learning): E-learning that takes place through portable electronic devices like smartphones and tablets.

Monetization: The process of earning revenue from your video content, often through advertising, sponsorships, or sales.

Multimedia Content: Content that uses a combination of different content forms such as text, audio, images, animations, or video. Essential in the creation of engaging course videos.

Natural Language Processing (NLP): A branch of AI that focuses on the interaction between computers and human language, particularly important in tools like Jasper.

Online Course Monetization: Strategies used to generate revenue from online courses.

Pay-Per-Click (PPC): A digital marketing model where advertisers pay a fee each time one of their ads is clicked.

Podcasting: The practice of using digital audio files made available on the Internet for downloading, often a part of content strategy in digital marketing and e-learning.

Resolution: The amount of detail that a video contains, typically measured in pixels (e.g., 1080p, 4K).

Responsive Design: The practice of designing web content to automatically adjust for optimal viewing on any device, from desktops to smartphones.

Royalty-Free Music: Music that can be used without paying

royalties for each use, often used as background tracks in videos.

Royalty-Free: This refers to content that can be used without paying royalties or licensing fees for each use.

Screen Recording Software: Tools used to capture the content displayed on a computer screen for video tutorials or presentations.

Search Engine Marketing (SEM): The practice of marketing a business using paid advertisements that appear on search engine results pages.

Search Engine Optimization (SEO): The practice of increasing the quantity and quality of traffic to your website through organic search engine results.

Speechify: Text-to-speech tool for converting written text into spoken audio.

Storyboarding: The process of sketching out the sequence of events in your video, slide by slide or scene by scene.

Storyboarding in E-Learning: A method used for visualizing the e-learning experience, similar to storyboarding in video production but often focused more on educational content flow.

Text-to-Speech (TTS): Technology that converts written text into spoken voice output.

Thumbnail: A small image representing a video on a platform like YouTube.

Thumbnail Optimization: The process of designing an engaging thumbnail to increase the click-through rate of a video.

Transitions: Visual effects used to move smoothly from one scene or clip to another in a video.

User Experience (UX): The overall experience of a person using a product, especially in terms of how easy or pleasing it is to use.

Video Hosting Platform: A service where videos are uploaded and shared, like YouTube or Vimeo.

Video Scripting: The process of writing scripts for video content tailored to convey information effectively in a visual format.

Voice Acting: The art of performing voiceovers to represent a character or provide information to an audience relevant to TTS and video content.

Voice Modulation: Adjusting the pitch, tone, and speed of a voiceover to convey different emotions or emphases.

Voiceover: Narration in a video where the speaker is not seen.

Webinar: An online seminar or workshop, often used in e-learning and digital marketing for educational purposes or to promote products/services.

White Hat SEO: The use of optimization strategies, techniques, and tactics that focus on a human audience as opposed to search engines and completely follow search engine rules and policies.

References

Jasper

Website: https://www.jasper.ai/

Description: AI-powered tool for content ideation and scriptwriting.

Grammarly

Website: https://www.grammarly.com/

Description: AI writing assistant for grammar checking and plagiarism detection.

Canva

Website: https://www.canva.com/

Description: Graphic design tool used for creating visual content, including YouTube thumbnails.

Speechify

Website: https://www.speechify.com/

Description: Text-to-speech tool for converting written text into spoken audio.

Lumen5

Website: https://lumen5.com/

Description: AI-driven platform for turning text content into engaging videos.

DALL-E

Website: https://openai.com/dall-e-2/

Description: AI program by OpenAI that generates images from textual descriptions. Images in this book are from DALL-E.

About the Author

Simon Lee is passionate about raising awareness and taking advantage of the once-in-a-lifetime opportunity of the AI Revolution that is upon us.

He is a multi-domain experienced individual with an MBA from a reputable business school and professional qualifications, which include PMP, PMI-PBA, and PMI-ACP certifications from the Project Management Institute. For over 35 years, he navigated the complexities of corporate America, excelling in roles like Senior IT Project Manager, Senior Business Analyst, Senior Researcher, and VP of Finance.

However, beneath his corporate veneer lay a passionate researcher and writer. Even during his corporate tenure, he avidly pursued writing, focusing on genres close to his heart: self-help, health & wellness, the human potential, technology, history, business and politics - and now the AI revolution.

Now semi-retired, Simon (his pen name) has dedicated himself wholly to in-depth research, crafting insightful ebooks, and using AI-powered tools to optimize his productivity. A staunch health enthusiast, he's predominantly vegan and engages in daily physical activities, whether it's jogging, working out, or enjoying rides on his electric bike. Weekends sometimes find him at the beach, soaking in the sun alongside his wife.